Budget Bliss

Budget Bliss

Matthew Petchinsky

1

Budget Bliss: The Easy Path to Financial Freedom
By: Matthew Petchinsky

Disclaimer

Budget Bliss: The Easy Path to Financial Freedom is provided for **educational and informational purposes only**. The content of this book is not intended to serve as financial, legal, accounting, tax, or investment advice, nor should it be interpreted as a substitute for advice from a licensed financial advisor, certified public accountant, attorney, or other qualified professional.

All budgeting strategies, financial frameworks, examples, and suggestions presented in this book are general in nature and may not be suitable for every individual, household, or financial situation. Personal financial outcomes vary widely based on income, expenses, debt obligations, geographic location, employment stability, health considerations, economic conditions, and individual decision-making. The author makes no guarantees regarding financial improvement, debt reduction, savings growth, or wealth creation as a result of using the information contained herein.

The reader acknowledges that **financial freedom is a personal and situational journey**, and that any actions taken based on this book are done voluntarily and at the reader's own discretion and risk. The author and publisher expressly disclaim any liability for losses, damages, hardships, or adverse outcomes—financial or otherwise—that may arise directly or indirectly from the use, misuse, or interpretation of the material in this book.

Any references to budgeting tools, apps, methods, habits, or systems are provided solely for illustrative and educational purposes. Mention of specific products, services, or financial concepts does not constitute endorsement, sponsorship, or recommendation unless explicitly stated. The author does not receive compensation from any third-party tools or platforms mentioned unless otherwise disclosed.

This book may include forward-looking statements, motivational language, or aspirational examples intended to encourage financial mindfulness, responsibility, and empowerment. Such statements should not be interpreted as promises of future results. Past examples, hypothetical scenarios, or case illustrations do not guarantee similar outcomes.

By reading this book, the reader agrees to take **full responsibility for their financial decisions**, understands that personal finance involves risk, and acknowledges that no book, system, or method can replace individualized professional guidance when needed.

If you require personalized financial, tax, or legal advice, consult a qualified professional who can assess your specific circumstances.

Introduction

Money touches nearly every part of modern life—yet for something so central, it is rarely taught in a way that feels **calm, humane, and achievable**. For many people, finances are not just numbers on a spreadsheet; they are tangled with stress, shame, fear, exhaustion, and a lingering sense of never quite being "caught up." *Budget Bliss: The Easy Path to Financial Freedom* was written to gently untangle that knot.

This book does not begin with deprivation, rigid rules, or guilt-driven discipline. It begins with **relief**.

Budgeting is often portrayed as restriction—cutting joy, eliminating comfort, and living in constant self-denial. That approach fails not because people are lazy or irresponsible, but because it ignores how humans actually live, feel, and make decisions. True financial stability is not built through punishment. It is built through **clarity, compassion, and consistency**.

Budget Bliss offers a different path: one where budgeting becomes a supportive system rather than a source of anxiety. A system that works with your real life—not an idealized version of it. A system that is simple enough to maintain, flexible enough to survive setbacks, and powerful enough to quietly transform your financial future over time.

This book is designed for:

- People who feel overwhelmed by money but don't know where to start
- Those who have tried budgeting before and "failed"
- Anyone tired of financial advice that feels unrealistic, cold, or judgmental
- Readers who want peace, control, and confidence—not perfection

You will not be asked to track every penny obsessively, give up everything you enjoy, or overhaul your life overnight. Instead, you'll learn how to:

- Understand your money without fear
- Create a budget that feels light, realistic, and sustainable
- Replace financial chaos with gentle structure
- Build momentum through small, repeatable wins
- Shift your mindset from survival to stability—and eventually, freedom

Financial freedom is often marketed as something dramatic: sudden wealth, radical minimalism, or extreme hustle. In reality, it is far quieter—and far more attainable. It begins when your money stops surprising you. When bills are expected, not feared. When decisions feel intentional instead of reactive. When you trust yourself with money again.

That is the heart of Budget Bliss.

This book respects that everyone's circumstances are different. Income levels vary. Responsibilities differ. Health, family, geography, and opportunity all play a role. There is no one-size-fits-all solution here—only adaptable tools, grounding principles, and a steady path forward.

You are not behind.

You are not broken.

And you are not bad with money.

You simply haven't been given a system that honors both your humanity and your reality—until now.

Take a breath. Turn the page.

Your journey toward calmer money begins here.

Chapter 1: Simplifying Your Finances in 10 Minutes a Week

Financial peace does not require hours of spreadsheets, advanced math skills, or constant monitoring. In fact, the more complicated a system becomes, the more likely it is to be abandoned. This chapter introduces a radically gentle idea: **your entire financial life can be meaningfully supported with just ten intentional minutes each week**. Not ten minutes a day. Not constant tracking. Just ten focused minutes to maintain clarity, direction, and control.

What follows is not a rigid system, but a rhythm—one designed to fit into real life, fluctuating energy levels, and imperfect weeks. Simplification is not about doing less because you don't care; it's about doing less because you finally understand what actually matters.

Releasing the Myth of Constant Monitoring

Many people believe that financial responsibility means watching every dollar like a hawk. This belief often comes from financial advice culture that rewards hyper-vigilance and frames relaxation as recklessness. Over time, this creates anxiety, burnout, and avoidance rather than stability.

Constant monitoring trains your nervous system to associate money with threat. Every purchase feels dangerous. Every bill feels like a failure. Instead of empowering you, the system keeps you stuck in a loop of stress and self-criticism that makes consistency nearly impossible.

Financial health improves when your system supports calm awareness rather than fear-based control. You do not need to know everything at all times. You need **periodic clarity**, not constant surveillance.

Ten minutes a week works because it creates a predictable, low-pressure container. Your finances get attention regularly, but not obsessively. This consistency builds trust between you and your money.

When you release the myth that "more tracking equals more responsibility," you make space for a system that actually survives real life.

Defining What Truly Needs Attention

Not all financial details deserve equal focus. Some numbers change daily and offer little insight. Others shift slowly but define your stability. Simplification begins by separating **signal from noise**.

Your core financial anchors are simple: income, fixed expenses, flexible spending, and available margin. These are the elements that determine whether your system is working. Everything else is secondary.

Most financial stress comes from paying attention to the wrong things. People obsess over small discretionary purchases while ignoring structural issues like subscription creep or misaligned bills. Simplification reverses this imbalance.

In your weekly ten minutes, you are not auditing your life. You are checking alignment. Are your bills covered? Are you staying within your flexible range? Has anything changed that needs adjustment?

By narrowing your focus to what truly matters, you stop drowning in details and start seeing your financial life clearly for the first time.

Creating a Weekly Financial Anchor Ritual

A system only works if it becomes a habit. The easiest habits are tied to time, not mood. Your ten-minute weekly check-in works best when it happens on the same day, in the same general context, every week.

This is not a task—it's a ritual. A moment where you sit down, breathe, and reconnect with your financial reality without judgment. Lighting a candle, making tea, or playing calm music can help signal safety to your nervous system.

During this ritual, you are not fixing everything. You are simply observing. You glance at your balance, upcoming bills, and recent spending patterns. You notice without reacting.

This regular, gentle contact prevents money from becoming a looming unknown. When finances are acknowledged weekly, they stop ambushing you emotionally.

Over time, this ritual builds a quiet confidence. You know what's coming. You know where you stand. And that knowledge brings peace.

Designing a One-Page Financial Snapshot

Complex dashboards fail because they demand too much attention. A simplified system works because it fits on one page—physically or digitally—and can be reviewed in minutes.

Your one-page snapshot includes only what you need: total monthly income, fixed monthly expenses, flexible spending allowance, savings or buffer amount, and any upcoming irregular expenses. That's it.

This snapshot is not a detailed ledger. It is a map. It tells you where you are and where you're going without overwhelming you with terrain.

When your finances live on one page, avoidance disappears. You're no longer afraid to look because there's nothing intimidating there.

This snapshot becomes the centerpiece of your weekly ten minutes. It evolves slowly as your life changes, but its simplicity remains constant.

Letting Go of Perfection and "Catching Up"

Many people avoid simplifying because they believe they must first "catch up" or fix past mistakes. This belief keeps them stuck indefinitely. Simplification starts where you are—not where you wish you were.

You do not need to correct every error, repay every debt immediately, or understand every past transaction to move forward. Progress does not require retroactive perfection.

Your system begins today. This week. This ten-minute window. Everything before this moment is context, not condemnation.

Letting go of perfection allows your system to be flexible. Missed a week? You return the next. Overspent one category? You adjust calmly.

When perfection is removed, consistency becomes possible—and consistency is what creates lasting financial change.

Building Trust Through Gentle Consistency

Financial confidence is not built through intensity; it is built through reliability. Each week you show up for your ten minutes, you reinforce trust in yourself.

This trust compounds. Over time, you stop fearing your finances because you know you will meet them regularly. Money becomes something you manage, not something that controls you.

Gentle consistency also makes room for growth. Once your base is stable, you naturally begin to optimize—but only when it feels supportive, not forced.

Your financial system becomes a quiet background structure rather than a constant source of stress. That is the essence of simplification.

Ten minutes a week is not a limitation. It is a promise that your financial life can be both effective and humane.

Journal Prompts

1. What emotions come up when I think about checking my finances regularly?
2. Where did I learn the belief that budgeting must be complicated or stressful?
3. What would financial calm feel like in my body and daily life?
4. Which financial details truly matter for my stability right now?
5. What would make a weekly money check-in feel safe and supportive?
6. How has perfectionism affected my relationship with money?
7. What does consistency mean to me outside of pressure or guilt?
8. Where can I simplify rather than optimize at this stage of my journey?
9. How would my life change if money stopped surprising me?
10. What promise can I make to myself about gentle financial care?

Closing Reflection

Simplifying your finances is not about shrinking your life—it's about **creating space within it**. When money is no longer a constant mental burden, energy returns to your relationships, creativity, health, and sense of agency.

This chapter invites you to trust that small, steady attention is enough. Ten minutes a week may seem insignificant, but consistency transforms it into a powerful foundation. Financial freedom does not begin with dramatic change; it begins with calm presence.

By choosing simplicity, you choose sustainability. By choosing gentleness, you choose longevity. And by showing up weekly—even imperfectly—you begin building a financial life that supports you rather than drains you.

This is not the start of restriction.
It is the start of ease.

Chapter 2: Budget Hacks for Everyday Savings

Saving money does not require extreme frugality, coupon obsession, or sacrificing everything that makes life enjoyable. In fact, the most effective savings strategies are often subtle, quiet, and woven seamlessly into daily routines. This chapter focuses on **everyday budget hacks**—small, intelligent adjustments that reduce financial leakage without increasing mental load.

These strategies work because they respect reality. You still live your life. You still buy groceries, pay bills, and enjoy small pleasures. The difference is that your money begins to **stay with you longer**, building stability without strain.

Redefining Savings as Retention, Not Deprivation

Most people think of saving as something active and painful—setting money aside after resisting temptation. This framing makes saving feel like loss. In truth, savings are often created by **preventing money from slipping away unnoticed**.

Everyday savings are less about saying "no" and more about saying "not automatically." Automatic spending habits drain far more money than conscious choices ever do. Small leaks add up quietly over time.

When you reframe savings as retention, you stop feeling deprived. You're not giving something up—you're keeping what already belongs to you.

This shift reduces resistance. Instead of fighting yourself, you work with your natural behavior patterns. That cooperation is what makes savings sustainable.

The goal is not to live smaller. The goal is to live **intentionally**, with fewer regrets and more control.

Using Friction to Your Advantage

Modern spending is designed to be frictionless. One-click purchases, stored cards, and auto-renewals remove pause points that once protected your money. Budget hacks restore **healthy friction**.

Adding friction does not mean inconvenience—it means intention. Removing saved cards, delaying purchases by 24 hours, or requiring a manual transfer creates space for conscious choice.

Most impulse spending fades when given time. Friction exposes what you truly want versus what was simply convenient.

This approach preserves willpower by eliminating the need for constant self-control. The system does the work for you.

By designing friction intentionally, you protect your finances without relying on motivation.

Optimizing Recurring Expenses Quietly

Recurring expenses are powerful because they repeat. Even small monthly charges become significant over a year. The most effective budget hacks target these quiet drains.

Subscriptions, insurance premiums, phone plans, utilities, and memberships often go unchecked for years. A single review can unlock immediate savings.

Negotiation, downgrading, or canceling unused services often yields more impact than cutting daily pleasures. These changes are invisible once done.

Optimizing recurring costs creates permanent financial relief with minimal lifestyle disruption.

Once optimized, these savings continue automatically—no effort required.

Leveaging Timing and Cycles

When you buy often matters as much as what you buy. Aligning spending with natural cycles creates savings without sacrifice.

Grocery planning around weekly sales, seasonal purchasing, and bulk buying for staples reduces costs effortlessly over time.

Delaying non-urgent purchases until sales periods preserves cash without denying enjoyment.

Timing-based hacks feel gentle because they don't remove pleasure—they simply **shift it**.

This patience compounds into significant long-term savings.

Designing Spending Buckets That Absorb Reality

Rigid budgets break when life happens. Flexible spending buckets succeed because they anticipate variability.

Instead of micromanaging categories, you allocate ranges. Some weeks you spend more. Other weeks you don't. The bucket absorbs fluctuation.

This approach reduces guilt and eliminates the "budget failure" mindset. Overspending becomes data, not judgment.

When systems forgive, people stay consistent.

Savings grow naturally when pressure disappears.

Turning Awareness into Automatic Wins

The best budget hacks eventually disappear into the background. Awareness creates the change, then automation preserves it.

Once patterns are adjusted—subscriptions trimmed, friction added, timing optimized—the system maintains itself.

This frees mental energy. Money stops demanding attention because it's no longer leaking.

Savings become a byproduct of alignment, not effort.

Financial ease emerges quietly, week by week.

Journal Prompts

1. Where does my money most often leave without conscious choice?
2. Which purchases feel automatic rather than intentional?
3. How do I emotionally associate saving—with loss or with relief?
4. Which recurring expenses deserve review this month?
5. What kind of friction would help me pause without frustration?
6. Where could timing reduce costs without reducing joy?
7. How does guilt affect my budgeting behavior?
8. What would a forgiving financial system look like for me?
9. Which savings strategies feel supportive rather than restrictive?
10. How would my stress change if savings happened quietly in the background?

Closing Reflection

Everyday savings are not built through intensity—they are built through **alignment**. When your systems match how you live, money begins to cooperate instead of resist.

These budget hacks work because they honor your humanity. They do not ask you to become someone else. They simply help you stop bleeding value in places you never meant to.

As savings accumulate quietly, confidence grows. The urgency fades. Decisions become easier. Money shifts from enemy to ally.

This chapter is not about cutting back.

It is about **keeping more of what already passes through your hands**—with ease, dignity, and calm.

Chapter 3: Paying Off Debt Faster Without Stress

Debt is rarely just a math problem. It carries emotional weight—shame, fear, frustration, and the constant pressure of "catching up." Many people know *what* they should do to pay off debt, yet feel frozen by the stress of actually doing it. This chapter is designed to change that experience.

Paying off debt does not require panic, punishment, or extreme sacrifice. In fact, stress is often the very thing that slows progress. Sustainable debt reduction comes from **clarity, compassion, and structure**, not fear. When stress is removed, momentum becomes possible.

Reframing Debt as a System, Not a Moral Failure

Debt is often treated as evidence of irresponsibility or lack of discipline. This framing is deeply damaging and rarely accurate. Most debt is created through survival, education, medical needs, family obligations, or systemic pressures—not personal failure.

When debt is moralized, people avoid it mentally. Statements are unopened. Balances are ignored. Shame delays action far more than numbers ever could.

Debt is simply a system: borrowed money with rules attached. Systems can be understood, managed, and optimized—without judgment.

Once debt is neutralized emotionally, it becomes workable. You move from self-blame to problem-solving.

Freedom begins when you stop punishing yourself and start organizing your reality.

Choosing a Strategy That Fits Your Nervous System

The "best" debt payoff strategy is the one you can actually sustain. Some people thrive on aggressive payoff plans. Others shut down under pressure. Both responses are valid.

Debt snowball methods prioritize emotional wins. Avalanche methods prioritize mathematical efficiency. Hybrid approaches balance both. None are universally superior.

What matters is nervous system compatibility. A plan that creates dread will fail, no matter how logical it looks on paper.

Stress-free progress comes from choosing a strategy that feels manageable, predictable, and humane.

Your system should calm you—not demand heroics.

Creating a Minimum-Plus Framework

One of the most effective ways to reduce debt without stress is the **minimum-plus** approach. You commit to paying the minimum required on all debts, then add a small, consistent "plus" amount to one targeted balance.

The plus amount is intentionally modest. It should feel easy, not heroic. This removes fear of failure and builds consistency.

Over time, this extra payment creates real momentum. Progress happens quietly but steadily.

As confidence grows, the plus can increase naturally—without pressure.

Debt shrinks faster when your system encourages showing up rather than burning out.

Reducing Interest Drag Before Increasing Effort

Interest is the invisible force that makes debt feel endless. Reducing interest often matters more than increasing payment size.

Negotiating rates, consolidating balances, refinancing, or transferring to lower-interest options can dramatically accelerate payoff without additional stress.

These actions are one-time efforts that produce long-term relief. Once done, they require no ongoing willpower.

Lower interest means more of your money goes toward progress rather than maintenance.

This shift alone can restore hope and motivation.

Protecting Stability While Paying Down Debt

Many people sabotage debt progress by neglecting stability. Without a buffer, any unexpected expense triggers new debt, undoing progress.

Even a small emergency cushion prevents regression. Stability is not a reward—it is a prerequisite.

Paying off debt while remaining financially fragile creates constant anxiety. A stress-free system protects both progress and peace.

You are not "failing" by prioritizing stability alongside payoff.

You are building a system that lasts.

Letting Momentum Replace Pressure

Pressure creates short bursts of effort. Momentum creates lasting change. Debt payoff accelerates when progress feels encouraging rather than exhausting.

Celebrating small reductions, tracking progress visually, and acknowledging consistency builds positive feedback loops.

Momentum changes your identity. You stop being "someone with debt" and start being "someone actively reducing it."

This identity shift is powerful. It replaces dread with confidence.

Debt does not disappear overnight—but it loses its power over you long before the balance hits zero.

Journal Prompts

1. What emotions do I associate most strongly with debt?
2. Where did I learn to judge myself for having debt?
3. Which payoff approach feels calming rather than intimidating?
4. What would "stress-free progress" look like for me?
5. How does pressure affect my financial decision-making?
6. Where could a minimum-plus approach fit into my life?
7. What stability do I need in order to feel safe paying off debt?
8. How might reducing interest change my experience emotionally?
9. What small win would help me feel momentum this month?
10. Who am I becoming as I take consistent action?

Closing Reflection

Debt loses its power when it is no longer fueled by fear. The moment you approach it with structure and compassion, it becomes manageable—and then temporary.

This chapter is not about speed for its own sake. It is about creating a process that allows you to breathe while making progress. When stress is removed, clarity returns. When clarity returns, confidence grows.

You do not need to suffer to be responsible.
You do not need punishment to make progress.

By choosing calm, consistent action, you reclaim control—step by step—until debt becomes something you are leaving behind, not something you are defined by.

Chapter 4: Building Wealth Through Simple Investments

Wealth is often portrayed as complex—something reserved for experts, insiders, or those willing to take constant risks. This belief keeps many people on the sidelines, convinced they must master everything before starting. In reality, long-term wealth is built through **simplicity, patience, and consistency**, not constant action or advanced knowledge.

This chapter is not about chasing trends, day trading, or timing the market perfectly. It is about understanding how simple investments work, why they grow over time, and how to participate in wealth-building **without stress, overwhelm, or obsession**.

Redefining Wealth as a Long-Term Process

Many people imagine wealth as a sudden event: a windfall, a breakout investment, or a dramatic lifestyle shift. This expectation creates impatience and discouragement. True wealth, however, is almost always gradual.

Long-term investing works because it aligns with time rather than fighting it. Money grows not through constant effort, but through **allowing time to do the heavy lifting**.

When you view wealth as a process, pressure disappears. You stop needing immediate proof that you're "doing it right" and start trusting the system.

This mindset shift protects you from impulsive decisions driven by fear or excitement.

Wealth becomes something you build quietly, not something you chase loudly.

Understanding the Power of Compounding

Compounding is one of the simplest and most powerful forces in investing. It occurs when your returns begin generating returns of their own.

At first, growth appears slow—almost invisible. This early stage discourages many people into quitting too soon.

Over time, compounding accelerates. The same contribution produces dramatically larger results simply because it has had longer to grow.

Consistency matters more than size. Small, regular investments often outperform sporadic large ones.

Compounding rewards patience—not perfection.

Keeping Investments Boring on Purpose

Boring investments are often the most effective. Broad-based funds, diversified portfolios, and long-term holdings lack excitement—but they offer reliability.

Complex strategies increase risk, stress, and the likelihood of emotional decisions. Simplicity reduces mistakes.

A boring system requires fewer decisions, which protects you from reacting to short-term market noise.

When investments are boring, your life stays calm. You are less tempted to interfere.

Boring is not a flaw—it is a feature.

Automating Wealth to Remove Emotion

Emotions are the greatest threat to long-term investing success. Fear causes people to sell low. Excitement causes them to buy high.

Automation removes emotion by turning investing into a background process. Money moves consistently without requiring constant decisions.

Automatic contributions ensure participation during both good and bad market conditions.

This consistency smooths out volatility over time.

The less you touch your investments, the better they tend to perform.

Aligning Risk With Your Capacity for Calm

Risk is not just mathematical—it is emotional. A strategy that looks good on paper may fail if it causes constant anxiety.

Your ideal investment approach should allow you to sleep well at night. Calm investors stay invested longer.

Risk tolerance is personal and changes over time. There is no correct level—only what is sustainable for you.

Choosing calm over maximum returns often leads to better outcomes long-term.

Staying invested matters more than optimizing endlessly.

Letting Wealth Grow Quietly in the Background

Wealth grows best when it is not constantly watched. Obsessive checking amplifies fear during downturns and excitement during peaks.

Long-term investing thrives on **detachment and trust**.

When you focus on living your life while your investments quietly work, stress decreases and consistency improves.

Your role is not to manage growth daily—it is to **protect the process**.

Wealth accumulates while you focus on what matters most.

Journal Prompts

1. What beliefs do I currently hold about wealth and investing?
2. How do fear or excitement influence my financial decisions?
3. What does “boring but effective” mean to me?
4. How comfortable am I with letting time work for me?
5. What level of risk allows me to feel calm and confident?
6. Where might automation reduce stress in my financial life?
7. How does patience show up—or not show up—in my money habits?
8. What would change if I stopped checking progress constantly?
9. How do I define wealth beyond numbers alone?
10. What kind of future am I quietly building right now?

Closing Reflection

Building wealth does not require constant action—it requires **trust in simple systems and respect for time**. When investing becomes calm, consistent, and automated, it stops competing with your life and starts supporting it.

This chapter is an invitation to step out of urgency and into alignment. You do not need to outsmart the market. You need to participate in it steadily and patiently.

Wealth grows when you allow it to.
Quietly. Reliably. Over time.

And as your investments compound in the background, so does something just as valuable—your confidence in your ability to build a future without sacrificing your peace.

Chapter 5: Making Money Fun and Rewarding

For many people, money has become synonymous with stress, obligation, and fear. Bills arrive, numbers demand attention, and finances feel like something to endure rather than engage with. This chapter invites a radical shift: **money does not have to feel heavy to be handled responsibly**. In fact, when money becomes enjoyable, consistency and progress become far easier.

Making money fun is not about irresponsibility or denial of reality. It is about redesigning your relationship with money so that it motivates, rewards, and supports you instead of draining you. Joy is not the enemy of financial health—it is often the missing ingredient.

Releasing the Belief That Money Must Feel Serious

Many people subconsciously believe that if money feels light or enjoyable, they are not taking it seriously enough. This belief creates unnecessary tension and self-punishment.

Seriousness is not the same as effectiveness. In fact, systems that feel grim are more likely to be avoided. Avoidance causes more financial harm than playfulness ever could.

When money is allowed to feel approachable, people interact with it more often—and more honestly.

Enjoyment increases engagement. Engagement increases awareness. Awareness improves outcomes.

Financial responsibility does not require emotional suffering.

Gamifying Progress Without Creating Pressure

Games work because they provide feedback, milestones, and a sense of forward movement. Money systems benefit from the same principles.

Tracking progress visually—through charts, color coding, or progress bars—turns abstract numbers into something tangible and motivating.

Small wins matter. Celebrating debt reductions, savings milestones, or streaks of consistency reinforces positive behavior.

The key is gentle gamification, not competition or perfection. The game should encourage curiosity, not judgment.

When progress feels rewarding, momentum builds naturally.

Creating Personal Rewards That Reinforce Growth

Rewards do not undermine discipline—they sustain it. When used intentionally, rewards help associate positive emotions with responsible behavior.

The most effective rewards are aligned with your values and budget. They don't sabotage progress—they acknowledge it.

Rewards can be experiential rather than financial: time, rest, creativity, or enjoyment.

When milestones are paired with meaningful rewards, motivation shifts from obligation to anticipation.

Money becomes a tool for supporting life—not just maintaining it.

Designing Money Rituals That Feel Good

Rituals transform tasks into experiences. A money ritual might include music, comfort, or intentional calm.

These rituals reduce anxiety and signal safety to your nervous system. Money stops triggering stress responses.

When financial check-ins feel comforting, avoidance disappears.

Over time, these rituals build a sense of trust and familiarity with your financial life.

Money becomes something you meet with presence, not dread.

Aligning Money With Identity and Values

Money becomes rewarding when it reflects who you are and what you care about. When spending aligns with values, guilt decreases.

Values-based spending creates satisfaction that lasts longer than impulse purchases.

This alignment turns money into an expression of identity rather than a source of conflict.

When money supports what matters, progress feels meaningful—not hollow.

Purpose adds depth to financial success.

Letting Joy Sustain Long-Term Success

Financial systems fail when they rely on willpower alone. Joy sustains where discipline exhausts.

Enjoyable systems are repeated. Repetition creates results.

By making money rewarding, you increase your capacity for consistency over time.

Financial freedom is not built through misery—it is built through sustainable engagement.

When money feels supportive, you stop fighting it.

Journal Prompts

1. How do I emotionally experience money right now?
2. Where did I learn that money must feel stressful?
3. What would make financial progress feel enjoyable?
4. How do I respond to rewards versus pressure?
5. What rituals help me feel calm and focused?
6. How could I celebrate progress without overspending?
7. What values do I want my money to reflect?
8. When do I feel most motivated financially?
9. How does joy affect my consistency?
10. What would a playful relationship with money look like?

Closing Reflection

Money does not need to be feared to be respected. When financial systems invite joy, engagement increases and resistance fades.

This chapter is an invitation to soften your approach without weakening your results. Fun does not diminish discipline—it strengthens it.

By allowing money to feel rewarding, you build a relationship that lasts. One rooted not in control, but in collaboration.

Financial freedom is not only about numbers.
It is also about **how it feels to live with them**.

When money supports joy, growth follows naturally—and stays.

Appendix A: Budget and Savings Trackers

This appendix is designed to turn insight into action. Budgeting concepts only create change when they are **captured, tracked, and revisited**—but tracking does not need to be complicated to be effective. The trackers in this appendix are intentionally simple, flexible, and human-centered. They are meant to support awareness, not perfection.

You can use these trackers digitally, in a notebook, printed as worksheets, or adapted into a system that fits your lifestyle. There is no "correct" format—only what you will actually return to consistently.

How to Use These Trackers Without Burnout

Before diving in, it's important to release the idea that trackers must be filled out perfectly or daily. These tools are not surveillance systems. They are **checkpoints**.

You are encouraged to:

- Update weekly, not obsessively
- Skip weeks without guilt and resume calmly
- Adjust categories as your life changes
- Use estimates when exact numbers feel overwhelming

Trackers are meant to clarify patterns, not judge behavior. Their purpose is to support your ten-minute weekly financial rhythm, not replace it.

Tracker 1: Monthly Budget Snapshot

This tracker provides a one-page overview of your financial structure. It is the foundation of your entire system.

Sections to Include:

- Total Monthly Income
- Fixed Expenses (rent, utilities, insurance, phone, subscriptions)
- Flexible Spending Allowance (groceries, gas, personal spending)
- Savings Contribution
- Debt Payments
- Monthly Margin (what remains after essentials)

This snapshot answers one critical question:

Does my money support my life as it currently exists?

Update this once per month or whenever income or major expenses change.

Tracker 2: Weekly Money Check-In Log
This tracker supports consistency without micromanagement.
Weekly Prompts:

- Current account balance (approximate is fine)
- Bills paid this week
- Bills coming up next week
- Notable spending patterns
- One small win
- One adjustment (if needed)

This log keeps money from becoming invisible or intimidating. It builds trust through regular contact.

You are not solving everything here—you are staying oriented.

Tracker 3: Flexible Spending Tracker

Rather than tracking every purchase, this tracker focuses on **ranges and awareness.**

Suggested Format:

- Weekly flexible spending limit
- Actual spending (estimate)
- Difference (+ / –)
- Notes (no judgment)

This tracker helps you notice trends without emotional overload. Overages are not failures—they are information.

Over time, this tracker teaches you what your real-life spending needs actually are.

Tracker 4: Savings Growth Tracker
Savings grow best when progress is visible.
Sections:

- Starting balance
- Weekly or monthly contribution
- New balance
- Milestones reached
- Notes or reflections

Visualizing savings growth builds motivation and security. Even small increases matter.

This tracker reinforces the idea that savings are being **built**, not withheld.

Tracker 5: Emergency Buffer Tracker
Stability is the backbone of financial calm.
Track:

- Target buffer amount
- Current buffer balance
- Percentage complete
- Last contribution date

This tracker reminds you that safety is not optional—it is foundational.

Seeing your buffer grow reduces anxiety and prevents future debt.

Tracker 6: Debt Progress Tracker

Debt tracking should encourage momentum, not shame.

Suggested Fields:

- Creditor name
- Starting balance
- Interest rate
- Minimum payment
- Extra payment ("plus")
- Current balance
- Progress marker

This tracker helps you witness progress even when balances feel slow to change.

Progress tracked is progress felt.

Tracker 7: Subscription and Recurring Expense Review
This tracker prevents quiet financial leaks.
Review Quarterly:

- Service name
- Monthly cost
- Frequency of use
- Keep / downgrade / cancel decision
- Notes

One review can permanently lower expenses with no ongoing effort. This tracker pays for itself repeatedly.

Tracker 8: Annual Savings Goals Planner
Long-term goals provide direction without pressure.
Include:

- Goal name
- Target amount
- Timeframe
- Monthly contribution
- Why this goal matters

This planner connects money to meaning, which increases commitment.

Savings tied to purpose are easier to sustain.

Tracker 9: Financial Wins & Celebrations Log

This tracker reinforces positive behavior.

Log:

- Date
- Win (large or small)
- How it felt
- Reward or acknowledgment

Wins build identity. Identity sustains behavior.

This tracker trains your brain to associate money with progress rather than stress.

Tracker 10: Money Reflection Journal

Numbers alone do not capture the full story.

Reflection Prompts:

- What felt supportive this month?
- What felt stressful—and why?
- What worked better than expected?
- What needs gentler structure?
- What am I proud of?

This journal transforms budgeting from a task into a relationship. Reflection deepens self-trust.

Closing Reflection

These trackers are not meant to control you—they are meant to **support you**. Use them lightly. Adapt them freely. Abandon any that feel heavy and keep those that feel grounding.

Financial systems only work when they respect the human using them.

Your progress is not measured by perfect logs or flawless months. It is measured by your willingness to return, adjust, and continue.

Let these trackers serve as quiet companions on your path toward budget bliss—steady, forgiving, and always available when you need clarity.

Message from the Author:

I hope you enjoyed this book, I love astrology and knew there was not a book such as this out on the shelf. I love metaphysical items as well. Please check out my other books:

-Life of Government Benefits

-My life of Hell

-My life with Hydrocephalus

-Red Sky

-World Domination:Woman's rule

-World Domination:Woman's Rule 2: The War

-Life and Banishment of Apophis: book 1

-The Kidney Friendly Diet

-The Ultimate Hemp Cookbook

-Creating a Dispensary(legally)

-Cleanliness throughout life: the importance of showering from childhood to adulthood.

-Strong Roots: The Risks of Overcoddling children

-Hemp Horoscopes: Cosmic Insights and Earthly Healing

- Celestial Hemp Navigating the Zodiac: Through the Green Cosmos

-Astrological Hemp: Aligning The Stars with Earth's Ancient Herb

-The Astrological Guide to Hemp: Stars, Signs, and Sacred Leaves

-Green Growth: Innovative Marketing Strategies for your Hemp Products and Dispensary

-Cosmic Cannabis

-Astrological Munchies

-Henry The Hemp

-Zodiacal Roots: The Astrological Soul Of Hemp

- **Green Constellations: Intersection of Hemp and Zodiac**

-Hemp in The Houses: An astrological Adventure Through The Cannabis Galaxy

-Galactic Ganja Guide

Heavenly Hemp

Zodiac Leaves

Doctor Who Astrology

Cannastrology

Stellar Satvias and Cosmic Indicas

Celestial Cannabis: A Zodiac Journey

AstroHerbology: The Sky and The Soil: Volume 1

AstroHerbology:Celestial Cannabis:Volume 2

Cosmic Cannabis Cultivation

The Starry Guide to Herbal Harmony: Volume 1

The Starry Guide to Herbal Harmony: Cannabis Universe: Volume 2

Yugioh Astrology: Astrological Guide to Deck, Duels and more

Nightmare Mansion: Echoes of The Abyss

Nightmare Mansion 2: Legacy of Shadows

Nightmare Mansion 3: Shadows of the Forgotten

Nightmare Mansion 4: Echoes of the Damned

The Life and Banishment of Apophis: Book 2

Nightmare Mansion: Halls of Despair

Healing with Herb: Cannabis and Hydrocephalus

Planetary Pot: Aligning with Astrological Herbs: Volume 1

Fast Track to Freedom: 30 Days to Financial Independence Using AI, Assets, and Agile Hustles

Cosmic Hemp Pathways

How to Become Financially Free in 30 Days: 10,000 Paths to Prosperity

Zodiacal Herbage: Astrological Insights: Volume 1

Nightmare Mansion: Whispers in the Walls

The Daleks Invade Atlantis

Henry the hemp and Hydrocephalus

10X The Kidney Friendly Diet

Cannabis Universe: Adult coloring book

Hemp Astrology: The Healing Power of the Stars

Zodiacal Herbage: Astrological Insights: Cannabis Universe: Volume 2

Planetary Pot: Aligning with Astrological Herbs: Cannabis Universes: Volume 2

Doctor Who: Convergence Protocol – The Replicator War

Nightmare Mansion: Curse of the Blood Moon

The Celestial Stoner: A Guide to the Zodiac

Cosmic Pleasures: Sex Toy Astrology for Every Sign

Hydrocephalus Astrology: Navigating the Stars and Healing Waters

Lapis and the Mischievous Chocolate Bar

Celestial Positions: Sexual Astrology for Every Sign

Apophis's Shadow Work Journal: **:** A Journey of Self-Discovery and Healing

Kinky Cosmos: Sexual Kink Astrology for Every Sign

Digital Cosmos: The Astrological Digimon Compendium

Stellar Seeds: The Cosmic Guide to Growing with Astrology

Apophis's Daily Gratitude Journal

Cat Astrology: Feline Mysteries of the Cosmos

The Cosmic Kama Sutra: An Astrological Guide to Sexual Positions

Unleash Your Potential: A Guided Journal Powered by AI Insights

Whispers of the Enchanted Grove

Cosmic Pleasures: An Astrological Guide to Sexual Kinks

369, 12 Manifestation Journal

Whisper of the nocturne journal(blank journal for writing or drawing)

The Boogey Book

Locked In Reflection: A Chastity Journey Through Locktober

Generating Wealth Quickly:How to Generate $100,000 in 24 Hours

Star Magic: Harness the Power of the Universe

The Flatulence Chronicles: A Fart Journal for Self-Discovery

The Doctor and The Death Moth

Seize the Day: A Personal Seizure Tracking Journal

The Ultimate Boogeyman Safari: A Journey into the Boogie World and Beyond

Whispers of Samhain: 1,000 Spells of Love, Luck, and Lunar Magic: Samhain Spell Book

Apophis's guides:Witch's Spellbook Crafting Guide for Halloween

Frost & Flame: The Enchanted Yule Grimoire of 1000 Winter Spells

The Ultimate Boogey Goo Guide & Spooky Activities for Halloween Fun

Harmony of the Scales: A Libra's Spellcraft for Balance and Beauty

The Enchanted Advent: 36 Days of Christmas Wonders

Nightmare Mansion: The Labyrinth of Screams

Harvest of Enchantment: 1,000 Spells of Gratitude, Love, and Fortune for Thanksgiving

The Boogey Chronicles: A Journal of Nightly Encounters and Shadowy Secrets

The 12 Days of Financial Freedom: A Step-by-Step Christmas Countdown to Transform Your Finances

Sigil of the Eternal Spiral Blank Journal

A Christmas Feast: Timeless Recipes for Every Meal

Holiday Stress-Free Solutions: A Survival Guide to Thriving During the Festive Season

Yu-Gi-Oh! Holiday Gifting Mastery: The Ultimate Guide for Fans and Newcomers Alike

Holiday Harmony: A Hydrocephalus Survival Guide for the Festive Season

Celestial Craft: The Witch's Almanac for 2025 – A Cosmic Guide to Manifestations, Moons, and Mystical Events

Doctor Who: The Toymaker's Winter Wonderland

Tulsa King Unveiled: A Thrilling Guide to Stallone's Mafia Masterpiece

Pendulum Craft: A Complete Guide to Crafting and Using Personalized Divination Tools

Nightmare Mansion: Santa's Eternal Eve

Starlight Noel: A Cosmic Journey through Christmas Mysteries

The Dark Architect: Unlocking the Blueprint of Existence

Surviving the Embrace: The Ultimate Guide to Encounters with The Hugging Molly

The Enchanted Codex: Secrets of the Craft for Witches, Wiccans, and Pagans

Harvest of Gratitude: A Complete Thanksgiving Guide

Yuletide Essentials: A Complete Guide to an Authentic and Magical Christmas

Celestial Smokes: A Cosmic Guide to Cigars and Astrology

Living in Balance: A Comprehensive Survival Guide to Thriving with Diabetes Insipidus

Cosmic Symbiosis: The Venom Zodiac Chronicles

The Cursed Paw of Ambition

Cosmic Symbiosis: The Astrological Venom Journal

Celestial Wonders Unfold: A Stargazer's Guide to the Cosmos (2024-2029)

The Ultimate Black Friday Prepper's Guide: Mastering Shopping Strategies and Savings

Cosmic Sales: The Astrological Guide to Black Friday Shopping

Legends of the Corn Mother and Other Harvest Myths

Whispers of the Harvest: The Corn Mother's Journal

The Evergreen Spellbook

The Doctor Meets the Boogeyman

The White Witch of Rose Hall's SpellBook

The Gingerbread Golem's Shadow: A Study in Sweet Darkness

The Gingerbread Golem Codex: An Academic Exploration of Sweet Myths

The Gingerbread Golem Grimoire: Sweet Magicks and Spells for the Festive Witch

The Curse of the Gingerbread Golem

10-minute Christmas Crafts for kids

Christmas Crisis Solutions: The Ultimate Last-Minute Survival Guide

Gingerbread Golem Recipes: Holiday Treats with a Magical Twist

The Infinite Key: Unlocking Mystical Secrets of the Ages

Enchanted Yule: A Wiccan and Pagan Guide to a Magical and Memorable Season

Dinosaurs of Power: Unlocking Ancient Magick

Astro-Dinos: The Cosmic Guide to Prehistoric Wisdom

Gallifrey's Yule Logs: A Festive Doctor Who Cookbook

The Dino Grimoire: Secrets of Prehistoric Magick

The Gift They Never Knew They Needed

The Gingerbread Golem's Culinary Alchemy: Enchanting Recipes for a Sweetly Dark Feast

A Time Lord Christmas: Holiday Adventures with the Doctor

Krampusproofing Your Home: Defensive Strategies for Yule

Silent Frights: A Collection of Christmas Creepypastas to Chill Your Bones

Santa Raptor's Jolly Carnage: A Dino-Claus Christmas Tale

Prehistoric Palettes: A Dino Wicca Coloring Journey

The Christmas Wishkeeper Chronicles

The Starlight Sleigh: A Holiday Journey

Elf Secrets: The True Magic of the North Pole

Candy Cane Conjurations

Cooking with Kids: Recipes Under 20 Minutes

Doctor Who: The TARDIS Confiscation

The Anxiety First Aid Kit: Quick Tools to Calm Your Mind

Frosty Whispers: A Winter's Tale

The Infinite Key: Unlocking the Secrets to Prosperity, Resilience, and Purpose

The Grasping Void: Why You'll Regret This Purchase

Astrology for Busy Bees: Star Signs Simplified

The Instant Focus Formula: Cut Through the Noise

The Secret Language of Colors: Unlocking the Emotional Codes

Sacred Fossil Chronicles: Blank Journal

The Christmas Cottage Miracle

Feeding Frenzy: Graboid-Inspired Recipes

Manifest in Minutes: The Quick Law of Attraction Guide

The Symbiote Chronicles: Doctor Who's Venomous Journey

Think Tiny, Grow Big: The Minimalist Mindset

The Energy Key: Unlocking Limitless Motivation

New Year, New Magic: Manifesting Your Best Year Yet

Unstoppable You: Mastering Confidence in Minutes

Infinite Energy: The Secret to Never Feeling Drained

Lightning Focus: Mastering the Art of Productivity in a Distracted World

Saturnalia Manifestation Magick: A Guide to Unlocking Abundance During the Solstice

Graboids and Garland: The Ultimate Tremors-Themed Christmas Guide

12 Nights of Holiday Magic

The Power of Pause: 60-Second Mindfulness Practices

The Quick Reset: How to Reclaim Your Life After Burnout

The Shadow Eater: A Tale of Despair and Survival

The Micro-Mastery Method: Transform Your Skills in Just Minutes a Day

Reclaiming Time: How to Live More by Doing Less
Chronovore: The Eternal Nexus
The Mind Reset: Unlocking Your Inner Peace in a Chaotic World
Confidence Code: Building Unshakable Self-Belief
Baby the Vampire Terrier
Baby the Vampire Terrier's Christmas Adventure
Celestial Streams: The Content Creator's Astrology Manual
The Wealth Whisperer: Unlocking Abundance with Everyday Actions
The Energy Equation: Maximize Your Output Without Burning Out
The Happiness Algorithm: Science-Backed Steps to Joyful Living
Stress-Free Success: Achieving Goals Without Anxiety
Mindful Wealth: The New Blueprint for Financial Freedom
The Festive Flavors of New Year: A Culinary Celebration
The Master's Gambit: Keys of Eternal Power
Shadowed Secrets: Groundhog Day Mysteries
Beneath the Burrow: Lessons from the Groundhog
Spring's Whispers: The Groundhog's Prediction
The Limitless Mindset: Unlock Your Untapped Potential
The Focus Funnel: How to Cut Through Chaos and Get Results
Bold Moves: Building Courage to Live on Your Terms
The Daily Shift: Simple Practices for Lasting Transformation
The Quarter-Life Reset: Thriving in Your 20s and 30s
The Art of Shadowplay: Building Your Own Personal Myth
The Eternal Loop: Finding Purpose in Repetition
Burrowing Wisdom: Life Lessons from the Groundhog
Shadow Work: A Groundhog Day Perspective
Love in Bloom: 5-Minute Romantic Gestures
The Shadowspell Codex: Secrets of Forbidden Magick
The Burnout Cure: Finding Balance in a Busy World
The Groundhog Prophecy: Unlocking Seasonal Secrets
Nog Tales: The Spirited History of Eggnog

Six More Weeks: Embracing Seasonal Transitions
The Lumivian Chronicles: Fragments of the Fifth Dimension
Money on Your Mind: A Beginner's Guide to Wealth
The Focus Fix: Breaking Through Distraction
January's Spirit Keepers: Mystical Protectors of the Cold
Creativity Unchained: Unlocking Your Wildest Ideas in 2025
Manifestation Mastery: 365 Days to Rewrite Your Reality
The Groundhog's Mirror: Reflecting on Change
The Weeping Angels' Christmas Curse
Burrowed in Time: A Groundhog Day Journey
Heartbeats: Poems to Share with Your Valentine
Dino Wicca: The Sacred Grimoire of Prehistoric Magick
Courage of the Pride: Finding Your Inner Roar
The Lion's Leap: Bold Moves for Big Results
Healthy Hustle: Achieving Without Overworking
Practical Manifesting: Turning Dreams into Reality in 2025
Jurassic Pharaohs: Unlocking the Magick of Ancient Egypt and Dino Wicca
The Happiness Equation: Small Changes for Big Joy
The Confidence Compass: Finding Your Inner Strength
Whispers in the Hollow: Tales of the Forgotten Beasts
Echoes from the Hollow: The Return of Forgotten Beasts
The Hollow Ascendant: The Rise of the Forgotten Beasts
The Relationship Reset: Building Better Connections
Mastering the Morning: How to Win the Day Before 8 AM
The Shadow's Dance: Groundhog Day Symbolism
Cupid's Kitchen: Quick Valentine's Day Recipes
Valentine's Day on a Budget: Love Without Breaking the Bank
Astrocraft: Aligning the Stars in the World of Minecraft
Forecasting Life: Groundhog Day Reflections
Bleeding Hearts: Twisted Tales of Valentine's Terror
Herbal Smoke Revolution: The Ultimate Guide to Nature's Cigarette Alternative

Winter's Wrath: The Complete Survival Blueprint for Extreme Freezes.

The Groundhog's Shadow: A Tale of Seasons

Burrowed Insights: Wisdom from the Groundhog

Sensual Strings: The Art of Erotic Bondage

Whispered Flames: Unlocking the Power of Fire Play

Forgotten Shadows: A Guide to Cryptids Lost to Time

Six Weeks of Secrets: Groundhog Day's Hidden Messages

Shadows and Cycles: Groundhog Day Reflections

The Art of Love Letters: Crafting the Perfect Message

Romantic Getaways at Home: Turning Your Space into Paradise

Purrfect Brews: A Cat Lover's Guide to Coffee and Companionship

The Groundhog's Wisdom: Timeless Lessons for Modern Life

The Shadow Oracle: Groundhog Day as a Predictor

Emerging from the Burrow: A Journey of Renewal

The Language of Love: Learning Your Partner's Love Style

Authorpreneur: The Ultimate Blueprint for Writing, Publishing, and Thriving as an Author

Weathering the Seasons: Groundhog Day Perspectives

Valentine's Day Magic: A Guide to Romantic Rituals

The Shadow Chronicles: Stories of Groundhog Day

Love and Laughter: Fun Games for Valentine's Day

AstroRealty: Unlocking the Stars for Property Success

The Groundhog's Path: A Guide to Seasonal Balance

Groundhog Day Diaries: Reflections in the Shadow

The Groundhog's Light: Illuminating the Path Ahead

Valentine's Traditions from Around the World

AI Wealth Revolution: Unlocking the Trillionaire Mindset

Love Rekindled: Reigniting Passion in Relationships

Single and Thriving: Self-Love on Valentine's Day

Emerald Legends: Mystical Tales of Ireland

Green Alchemy: Harnessing Nature's Magic
The Hearts of Horror: A Valentine's Day Nightmare
The Leprechaun's Guide to Wealth and Wisdom
Dancing with the Sidhe: Celebrating the Otherworld
Shamrocks and Shadows: Mysteries of the Green Isle
Emerald Energy: Harnessing Luck and Growth
The Gingerbread Golem's Valentine: A Sweetheart's Guide to Love and Enchantment
The Celtic Knot: Weaving Life and Destiny
Green Fire: Elemental Magic for St. Patrick's Day
Clover Chronicles: Finding Your Inner Luck
Ireland's Mystical Creatures: A Field Guide
Gingerbread Golem's Love Almanac
Prowl and Thrive: The Lion's Guide to Success
Love Alchemy: Transforming Your Life Through Heart Energy
WORLD DOMINATION: Woman's Rule 3:The New Life
The Midnight Rose: A Guide to Lunar Love Spells
The Forbidden Letters: Writing Your Own Love Prophecy
Luck and Lore: St. Patrick's Day for Modern Mystics
The Green Path: A Pagan Celebration of Renewal
The Dark Architect's Guide to Reprogramming Reality
Prankster's Paradise: A Guide to Harmless Hijinks
Manifest Your Reality: The Law of Attraction Simplified
The TARDIS Owner's Manual: Understanding the Doctor's Ship: *A complete guide to the TARDIS, its technology, secrets, and mysteries*
Starlit Romance: Astrology Secrets for Finding True Love
The Time Lord's Atlas: A Complete Guide to the Whoniverse: ***A breakdown of the locations, planets, and dimensions explored in Doctor Who***
Sweetheart Shadows: The Dark Side of Love and Attraction
February Fire: Reigniting Passion in Every Area of Life

The Self-Love Toolkit: 5 Ways to Embrace Who You Are
February Sparks: Ignite Your Dreams in 28 Days
March to Success: A 31-Day Action Blueprint
Ancient Paths: The 13 Sacred Principles of Dino Wicca
Echoes of Tomorrow: Navigating the AI Revolution
The Wellness Blueprint: Balancing Mind, Body, and Soul
Green Horizons: Sustainable Living for a Better Tomorrow
The AI Wealth Code: How to Make Millions with Automation
AI-Powered Creativity: Writing, Art, and Music for Profit
Extinction Rites: Rebirthing Your Soul Through Prehistoric Magick
Sacred Serpents tarot
Celestial Enchantment blank journal
Star Strains
Culinary Journeys: Exploring Global Flavors at Home
The Hollowvale Curse
The Hollowvale Harvest
The Egg of Transformation: Awakening Your Inner Power
Blooming Into Power: A Wiccan Guide to Spring Awakening
The Nightmare Nexus: The Third Doctor's Perilous Haunting
Digital Detox: Reclaiming Your Life in a Connected World
Ostara's Path: Walking the Spiral of Renewal
The Sacred Hare
Financial Freedom: Building Wealth in the Modern Age
Spring's Cauldron: Stirring the Waters of Change
The Hollowvale Pact
Quantum Consciousness: The Science of Reality Shifting
The Hollowvale Hunger
The Sacred Waters Within: A Witch's Guide to Hydrocephalus Magick
The Raven's Nest: Building a Life of Unshakable Stability
AI and the Human Mind: The Future of Intelligence
The Hollowvale Reckoning

Timeless Love: Building and Maintaining Lasting Relationships

The Raven's Roar: Unlocking Unstoppable Confidence

Raven Sight: Awakening Intuition and Inner Wisdom

The Butterfly Effect: Small Changes, Big Transformations

Taming the Boogeyman: How to Conquer Your Inner Fears

The Magick of Green: Awakening Earth's Energy in You

The Entrepreneurial Mindset: Secrets to Business Success

The Hollowvale End

The Shadow Luck Ritual: Reclaiming Power from Your Dark Side

Spring Magick for Beginners: A Simple Guide to Seasonal Energy Work

Doctor Who: The Hollowvale Conundrum

The March of Miracles: Unlocking Synchronicities in Spring

Unveiling the Cosmos: A Guide to Stargazing and Space Exploration

The Ultimate Guide to Surviving an Economic Collapse

The AI Gold Rush: How to Profit from the AI Revolution

Bastet's Shadow: The Hidden Power of Feline Magick

The Bastet Codex: Unlocking the Goddess's Magickal Secrets

Purring Spells: Harnessing Bastet's Healing Frequencies

Bastet's Nine Lives: Rebirth, Transformation, and Immortality Spells

Primal Currents: Hydrocephalus Magick in the Path of Dino Wicca

The Digital Gold Rush: Mastering E-Commerce and Online Sales

Future Shock: Adapting to the Next Decade of Change

The Quantum Mindset: Think Like a Billionaire

Sacred Motherhood: Awakening the Divine Feminine Within

The Mother's Spellbook: Enchantments for Love, Protection, and Prosperity

The Witch's Guide to Parenting: Raising Empowered and Intuitive Children

The Magick of Motherhood: Reclaiming Your Power Through Rituals

The Pagan Path to Self-Love: A Goddess's Guide to Worth and Confidence

Wild Woman Magick: Unleashing Your Primal Power

The Money Magnet Blueprint: Unlocking Unlimited Wealth

Biohacking 101: Unlock Your Body's Full Potential

The Wild Father: A Pagan Guide to Strength and Wisdom

The Sacred Masculine: Unlocking Your Inner Power

The Druid's Compass

The Warrior's Mindset

The Father's Fire

Odin's Path

Ancestral Bonds

The House That Whispers

The Magician's Code

The Wild Hunt

The Green Man's Path

The Altar of Success

The Shadow and the Sword

The High Priestess's Guide to Energy Healing

The Lunar Mother

The Sacred Self-Care Grimoire

The Womb Wisdom Codex

The Wheel of the Mother

The Witch's Guide to Manifestation

The Q2 Reset

The Ultimate Guide to AI-Powered Passive Income

Escape the 9-5

AI Feline Fortunes

The Tear-Stained Grimoire

Razorblade Runes
Cemetery Sirens
The Midnight Wristwatch
The Town That Forgets
AI Horror & Creepypasta
The Hollow Frequency
The Breach Echo
The Quiet Between Worlds
The Sigil of Tharan-Khul
Summon the Vault of Y'ha'ten
The Becoming Codex
The Profit of Az'ra-nar
The Drowned Logos
Echoes of the Eldritch Will
The Deep Ledger
Necronomicon of Networth
Covenant of the Wealthwyrm
The Whisperer's Manifesto
The Rites of Azh-K'luth
The Ark of the Crawling Coin
The Tithe of Shadows
Inkheart Abyss
The Timewinds of Y'ha-nthlei
The Spiral Labyrinth of Azag-Nirrh
The Gallifreyan Heresy of the Black Pharaoh
The Psalms of Nyog-Sotha
Black Rain Alchemy
The Infinite Maw
The Entropic Blueprint
The Oracle of Sh'guul
The Book of Breach
The Drowned Saint's Testament
Dreamcraft of the Sleeper God

The Silence Market
Cthonomics: The Dark Wealth Algorithm
Invocation of the Ten-Eyed King
Wealthbound to the Wyrm Below
Become the Unnameable
Codex of the Sovereign Flame
Rituals of Relentless Becoming
The Shadow Ascends
The Eyes Beneath You
The Will That Wakes Worlds
Silence Is a Weapon
The Mirror That Screams
The Whisper Between Moments
The Mind That Devours Fear
The Myth of the Finished Self
The Architect of Your Madness
The Voice You've Buried
The Discipline of Madness
Stormborn: Awakening Your Inner Tempest
The Mind That Ate Time
Unbind Your Becoming
The Pact You Owe Yourself
The Devourer's Diet
The Acid That Carves the Path
The Tower You Must Burn
The Breath Between Worlds
Speak Like the Deep
The Labyrinth Within
The Spine of the Sea God
Rejection Is a Portal
The Crown You Refused
The Scar Is the Spell
The Lightless Flame

The Habit of Becoming Horrific
ChickenJockey Chaos
The Gatekeeper Within
You Are Not Your Name
The Compass of the Mad
The Archive of Unsent Letters
What the Mirror Can't Show You
The Knife You Needed
Worship Nothing, Become Everything
The Other Voice
The Body the World Forgot
The Vein of the Void
The Black Bone Codex
The Puzzle of the Hidden Self (Millennium Puzzle)
The Eye That Sees the Lie *(Millennium Eye)*
The Ring of Return (Millennium Ring)
The Rod of Relentless Will ***(Millennium Rod)***
The Tally of the Soul (Millennium Tauk/Necklace)
The Key to the Locked Timeline (Millennium Key)
The Scale of Sacred Decisions (Millennium Scales)
Inferno Bites: The UnOfficial Minecraft Lava Cookbook
Rot in the Attic
Prana: The Hidden Force of Your Infinite Self
The Shadow Realm Within: Transforming Darkness Into Destiny
The Borderland Collapse
Claws of Protection: Bastet's Defensive Magick
Mr. Ring-a-Ding's Madness
Yugioh Astrology: Celestial Deckcraft and Duel Destiny (2026–2027 Edition)
The Seal You Signed: Unlocking the Power You Once Feared
The Puzzle of Infinite Minds: Unlocking the Mentalism Hidden Within

The Eye That Mirrors the All: Secrets of Inner Reflection
Doctor Who: The Toymaker's Broadcast
The Rod of Eternal Flow: Commanding the Currents of Vibration
Golden Eyes of Bastet: Enhancing Psychic Vision
The Key of Dual Forces: Balance Within the Polarity
The Scales of Living Rhythm: Timing the Dance of Life
The Necklace of Hidden Cause: Weaving the Webs of Fate
The Ring of Secret Masters: Rising Through the All Within All
Daggers of the Dying Deep
Bastet's Wealth and Fortune Magick: Prosperity Rituals of the Goddess
The Tide that Speaks
The Scrolls of Petosiris: 13 Rituals from the Feathered Eye
Petosiris and the Living Plague of Osirion
Feline Fire: Bastet's Passion and Love Magick
The Star Altar of Petosiris
Bastet's Whiskers: Supernatural Sensory Magick
The Bastet Grimoire
Feeding the Shadows
The Mouthless Prayer
The Spiral Wound
Becoming the Ibis: Lessons from Petosiris's Mind
The Crimson Coven: Cola Magick for Sweet Dominion
Sacred Cat's Paw
The Soda Zodiac: A Flavor for Every Sign
Covenant of the Crawling Flame
The Ink of Ish'Zur
Frothroot: The Thirst That Ate the World
The Golden Glyphs of Prosperity
The Etherbind Codex
Echoes of the Resistance: Reclaiming the You That Survived

Harnessed Minds: Breaking Free from Mental Control
The Eyes in the Smoke
Rootwake: The Carbon Covenant
Skitter Logic: Unlearning the Fear That Built You
Doctor Who: The World That Froths
Rootwake: The Fizz That Rewrites Flesh
Rootwake: Frothfather of the World
The Holly Pact: Blood Beneath the Mistletoe
The 2nd Mass Principle: Building Unbreakable Tribes
Web of Wits: A Survival Guide to Encounters with Anasi the Spider (Aunt Nancy)
The Hexbreaking Handbook: Effective Spells to Remove Curses
Pop Alchemy: Transform Your Life One Sip at a Time
The Mason Code: Leading in Unleadable Times
Petosiris and the Fifth Chamber of Thoth
The Ether Seed Within
The Parent of Tomorrow
Petosiris's Pyramid of Perpetual Wealth
Unlearn the World
Grimoire of the Hollow Tongue
Zodiac Weeds: Finding Your Strain Through the Stars
Aquarius Rises in the Bank
The Sugar God's Smile
The Skinclock Reversal: Biohacking the Face of Time
Debtburn: How to Obliterate What You Owe Forever
The Ice Cream Oracle: What Your Cone Says About Your Future
Silence Is Sovereignty: The Power of Being Unreadable
The Wind That Whispers Through Stone
Path of the Four Directions
Doctor Who: The Maestro's Symphony of Endings
Oxygen Grail: Breathing to Undo the Clock

Zodiacal Collapse: When Stars Devour Time
Teachings from the Red Sand Silence
Doctor Who: Omega – The Broken Equation
Memory Wipe Your Past: Start Over Like a MiB
Mitochondria Prime: Ignite the Core of Youth
A Nest of Roaches
Grub from the Galaxy: MiB Recipes You'll Never Forget
Whiskers of Power: Bastet's Guide to Inner Sovereignty
The Gift Must Cost Them: Negotiation Through Unequal Exchange
The Worm Guys' Wealth Code: Hustle Like an Alien
Bug Out: The Edgar Method for Ruthless Goal Setting
Weaving Life with Spiderwoman's Pattern
Doctor Who: The Rani's Renaissance
How to Get a Job (If You're a Puppygirl)
Speak Through Others: The Art of Proxy Power
T-Rex Your Trauma: Reclaim the Power of Your Primal Self
The Black Briefcase: How MiB Stay Wealthy in Silence
The Thirst Beyond Reason: Understanding Diabetes Insipidus From the Inside Out
Backwoods Witchcraft for Billionaires: The Pagan Path from Dirt Roads to Gold Roads
The Moonshine Grimoire: Fermented Spells for Abundance
The Nameless Geometry
The Wraith's Mixtape: Spellcasting with Songs of Sorrow
The Gallifreyan Gentleman: Silent Wealth, Sonic Confidence, and the Doctor's Code of Living
Sugar Water Confidence
Dino Totems: Spirit Guides from Earth's First Gods
Pumpkin Sigils & Ritual Smoke
The Hózhó Compass
The Distortus Discipline – Order from Inner Mutation
Witchcraft for the Cold-Blooded Soul

Moonlight Over the Blessingway
Water, Interrupted: When the Body Forgets How to Hold On
Deformed but Divine: Embracing Your Asymmetry
Hexes in the Henhouse: The Farm Witch's Guide to Power
The Reversed Flame: A Grimoire of Inverted Power
Salt, Cells, and Sanity: Reclaiming Balance with Diabetes Insipidus
King of the Broken: Crowning the Flawed Self
Moonlight Scars: Emo Moon Magick and the Art of Lunar Sorrow
Noose Spells: Magick of the Hanging Rope
The Goth Cathedral: Rituals of the Broken and Beautiful
The Cretaceous Codex: Dino Spirits and Fossil Magick
The Turkey Bones Ritual
Nine Lives of Manifestation: Unlocking Bastet's Reality Codes
Chaos Muscles: Building Strength from Twisted Pain
Emo Blood Magick: The Veins of Power
The 3AM Flood: Nighttime Urination, Sleep Loss, and the DI Spiral
The Silence Between the Stars
The Lemon Method: Sour Your Way to Success
Starlit Sovereign
The Rite of Twelve Gates: Walking the Gates of the Duat.
Cornbread and Conjure: Recipes for Riches and Rootwork
The Black Rose Rituals: Emo Love Spells and Obsession Magick
The Eternal Goodbye: Death Magick and Rebirth Rituals
Sinkrot: The Drain That Remembers
The Hybrid Mindset: Thinking Beyond Evolution
Bone Dry: Navigating Dehydration Before It Breaks You
Wreathcraft: Winter Sigils and Yuletide Spells
The Rite of Twelve Mouths

S'mores of the Damned: Haunted Recipes for Halloween Night

Rethink the Drink: A Beverage Survival Guide for DI Warriors

The Shadow Chord: Guitar Magick and Sonic

Malformed Yet Majestic: Leading When You Feel Wrong Inside

The Cursed Diary: Ink-Stained Spells of the Emo Soul

Anxiety Off Switch: Emergency Reset for a Fried Nervous System

The Energy Heist: How to Take Back Your Life from Drainers

Beyond the Bathroom: Rebuilding Your Social Life With DI

Coyote's Gift for Decision Makers

Ghoul-Goo: Spooky S'mores You'll Die For

Echoes in the Mirror: Scrying and Self-Destruction Magick

Thread and Thorn: Stitching Spells from Rural Cloth

The Mogwai Mind: Building Untouchable Wealth from Small Ideas

Be Your Own Guide: Trust Your Inner Compass

Hormones in Chaos: The Endocrine Puzzle of Diabetes Insipidus

ChronoCleanse: Detox Your Biological Timeline

The Limb You Hide Is the One That Saves You

Leaves, Bones, and Whisper Spells

The Dinosaur Mindset: Prehistoric Tactics for Modern Wealth

Clawing Back Control: A Bastet Method for Boundaries and Empowerment

Samhain Codes of the Forgotten

Orange Alchemy: The Autumnal Spellbook

Monster Within, Master Without

The Sigil That Sleeps

Hearthcraft: Yule Hearth Sigils and Winter Warmth Spells

Temple of the Purring Moon: Rituals from Bastet's Lineage
When the Earth Remembers Your Footsteps
Food for Mood: Eat to Heal Depression, Not Just Survive It
Witch of the Kudzu Vine: Southern Pagan Wealth Secrets
The Invisible Diagnosis: Advocating for Yourself With DI
The Coffin's Lullaby: Sleep Magick and Nightmares as Portals
Ashes of the Will: Rituals for Erasing the Self
The Fracture Rite: Shattering the Magickal Core
Funeral Candles: The Art of Emo Flame Magick
The Black Grimoire: A Blank Ritual for Writing in Absence
Phantom Thirst: A Halloween Survival Guide for Diabetes Insipidus
The Hollow Crown: Emo Royalty and Magick of the Outcast King
Sandpainting for the Soul
Falling Into Balance: Using the Extra Hour to Recalibrate Life
100 Southern Superstitions That Still Work
The DI Child: A Parent's Guide to Raising Hydrated, Happy Kids
The Jungle of Shame: Escaping the Hidden Lab of Doubt
The Witch's Toast: S'mores Spells and Creepy Confections
The Hoodoo Pantry: Spells from the Mason Jar
The Immortal Fortune: Secret Wealth Lessons from Captain Jack Harkness
The Specter's Embrace: Magick for Channeling Ghostly Lovers
Grateful Waters: A Thanksgiving Survival Guide for Diabetes Insipidus
The Seizure Gospel
Harvestbind: Autumn Sigils and Samhain Spells
Doctor Who: The Algorithmic Awakening
Silent Nights, Steady Waters: A Christmas Survival Guide for Diabetes Insipidus

The Extra Hour Effect: How One Hour Can Transform Everything

Blade Between the Breaths

Running with the Mountain Shadows

Echoes of the Failed Experiment – Becoming a Living Legacy

Swamp Witches & River Ghosts: Real Southern Hauntings

Cornbread Prophecies: Magical Recipes from a Southern Table

Doctor Who: The Signal in the Star

Bloomcraft: Spring Sigils and Equinox Enchantments

Vanisher: How to Disappear from the Internet Without Losing Your Life

The Ultimate Christmas Cookie Cookbook

The Unbreakable Parent: How to Mentally Survive Raising Kids in a Broken World

Time Debt: How to Reclaim the Hours You Didn't Know You Lost

One Month, One Million: Unconventional Cash Creation Tactics

Doctor Who: The Cyber Conversion Protocol

Black Friday Frenzy: The Art of Finding Hidden Online Deals

The Grimoire Buried Under the Apple Tree

Digital Couponing Masterclass: Your Step-by-Step Guide to Black Friday Savings

The Fire Inside the Flint

Shadows on the Ceiling: The Emo Guide to Astral Magick

The Bone-Eaters Beneath Us

Black Friday Bundle Blueprint: Creating Irresistible Product Packages for Maximum Sales

Thirteen Nights of Unbinding

Doctor Who: Engines of Influence

Pumpkin Spice Alchemy: Recipes of Fire and Frost

When Raptor Met Rexy: Prehistoric Lessons in Wild Romance
Oblivion's Candle: Burn the Path Behind You
Campfire Curses and Chocolate: A Halloween S'mores Grimoire
The Wallet That Wasn't Mine: Breaking Free from Inherited Scarcity
The Cola Zodiac: What Your Fizz Says About Your Fate
Frostfire Fortune: Unlocking Winter's Hidden Prosperity
Signal Jamming: Detox Your Brain from Info Overload
The Dust of the Forgotten Rite
The Golden Cat Sigils: Drawing Power in Bastet's Name
Mud Magick: The Prosperity of Getting Dirty
Savory Spicefall: Beyond the Pumpkin Pie
Pumpkin Spice Apothecary Kitchen
The Pumpkin Spice Economy: Turning Trends into Billions
The Ember Veil: 13 Nights of Fire Magick
Financial Freeze: When Earning Triggers Panic
The Gingerbread Alchemist: Sweet Recipes with a Twist
Biosynth Power: Programming Yourself from Scratch
Echoes from the Talking Circle
Truffle Alchemy: Fungus of Fortune
Spores of Power: The Truffle Witch's Handbook
Doctor Who: The Tower That Speaks
The Mycelium Veil: Truffle Magick Unbound
Broke But Ashamed: Healing the Shame Wound of Debt
The Evergreen Mind: Growth Through Winter Stillness
The Black Veil Truffle Rite
The Voice Beneath Symbols
Witchlight on the Bayou: Swamp Spells for Sovereignty
I Grew Up Poor and Now I Sabotage My Success
The Lantern of Hollow Souls

Shutdown Survival: A Citizen's Guide to Thriving When Government Stops

When Abundance Feels Like a Threat: Healing the Hidden Fears of Enough

The Scarecrow Grimoire

Owls of the October Veil

Candlewax and Curses: A Halloween Spellbook

Excavating the Inner Fossil – Transforming Fossilized Thoughtforms into Tools of Power

The Yule Witch's Spellbook: Magick for the Holiday Season

Haunted Christmas: Ghost Stories for Winter Nights

The Christmas Survival Guide: Thriving Through the Chaos

The Bone Orchard Rites

Haunted Commerce: The Ghost in the Marketplace

When Money Triggers the Inner Child

Silent Night with the Silence: A Christmas Thriller

The Lightning Crown: Living and Leading Through Seizures

TARDIS Tidings: Festive Stories from the Whoniverse

Autumn Reset: Slowing Down Without Falling Behind

The Trillion Dollar Soul: Rewriting the Currency of Reality

Truffle Eclipse Magick

Micro-Manifestations: Quick Magick That Works

5-Minute Rituals for Busy Witches

The Marshmallow Massacre: Halloween Treats with a Sinister Twist

Blood and Blackberry Thorns

Magickal Mornings: Rituals for a Blessed Christmas Day

Embers of the All-Hallows Fire

The Pumpkin Market Collapse

The Hour You Gained: Transforming Time Into Power

The Chamber Must Be Sealed: Mastering the Power of Controlled Access

The Cursed Manuscript of Petosiris

The Festive Hearth: Creating Holiday Traditions
Darkness Rising: Thriving as Nights Grow Longer
Harvesting Time: Turning the Year's End Into Your New Beginning
Petosiris and the 13th Zodiac Key
Wagewound: When Paychecks Become Identity Prisons
Walls That Watch
The Silent Feast: Rituals of Power in the Longest Night
The Distortus Legacy : Becoming a Deformed King in a Perfect World
The Hollow Masks
The Gratitude Furnace: Forging Gold from Thanks
Feast of Inner Gold: Eating for Energy and Enlightenment
Haunted Commerce: The Season of Spending Spirits
Fear Bonds: How Panic Creates Profit
Black Friday E-Commerce Playbook: Sales Tactics to Skyrocket Your Holiday Revenue
Budgeting for Black Friday: A Holiday Savings Planner
Haunting the Harvest Moon
The Warrior's Water: Emergency Preparedness for People With DI
The First Sip of the Year: A New Year's Survival Guide for Diabetes Insipidus
Doctor Who: The Thirteenth Node
The Unseen Struggle: Mental Health, Anxiety, and Chronic Thirst
The Hearth's Hidden Ledger: Counting Energies as Currency
The Gift Alchemist: Turning Any Offering Into Gold
The Papyrus of the Bound Spirit
The Magick of Leftovers: Transmutation in the Fridge
Frost and Fortune: Christmas Wealthcraft for the Modern Magus
Last-Minute Gifts: Creative Ideas on a Budget

10 Secrets to Surviving Holiday Crowds
The Witch's Dow Jones
The Witches' Graveyard Shift
Pumpkin Sigils: Carving Rites for Midnight Power
The Secret Shopper's Black Friday Guide: How to Get Early Access and VIP Deals
Fever in the Foundation
The Neuralyzer Reset: Reprogram Your Morning Routine
Lightning Lessons of the White Painted Woman
The Enchanted Snowflake
The Magic Sip: Surviving Disney Parks with Diabetes Insipidus
The One Who Draws Through You
Santa's Secrets: A Magical Holiday Planner
Silent Bells, Loud Miracles: Self-Help for the Season of Stillness
The Sugar Spell Codex: Confectionary Magick of Christmas
Autumn Hexcraft: Fallen Leaves, Fallen Barriers
Sleep Like a Fortress: Build a Life Where Insomnia Can't Survive
Nowhere Was Ever Home
Christmas Under the Stars: A Celestial Holiday Guide
Rentproof: How to Never Be Evicted Again
Workless: Escape the 9-5 Without Being Broke
The Gilded Gift: A Wealth Altar for Christmas Morning
The Black Friday Grimoire
The Hollowing: Ceremonies of Spiritual Collapse
Doctor Who: The Nameless Signal
Where the Eagle Hides His Courage
The Dwarf Tyrant's Ascent: Claiming Power in a World of Giants
The Currency of the Dead: Trading with Spectral Bankers
The Icebound Witch: Survival and Magick in the Cold

The Emergency Money Mind: Constant Crisis, Zero Calm

Thirst & Roses: A Valentine's Survival Guide for Diabetes Insipidus

Springing Into Clarity: Mastering the Energy Shift of Daylight Saving

Speed of the Nanotyrant: Agile Strategies for Life's Hunt

The 90-Day Reset: A Science-Backed Guide to Reinvent Yourself Before the New Year

The Coil of Thorns

Timegates Unleashed

Dopamine Fasting 2.0: Rewiring Your Brain in a World of Overstimulation

The Nanotyrannus Mutation: Embracing Your Differentiated Form

Unwritten January: How to Use the Blank Page of the Year to Re-Author Your Life

Feast of the Forgotten Spirits: Ancestor Magick for the Holidays

The Burnout Codex: A System for Thriving Beyond Stress

I Don't Deserve to Have Money

When the King Doesn't See You: The Shadow Predator's Guide

The Reset Ritual :A Guide to Shedding Last Year's Weight—Emotional and Physical—by Spring Cleaning Your Soul

Calendar Alchemy: Learn to Bend Time and Productivity around Your Natural Rhythms

The Mirror Contract: A One-Sentence Agreement with Yourself that Unlocks Real Change

The Nile Formula: Sacred Flow for Millionaire Minds

Forward Momentum: Productivity Rituals for the Lost Hour

Harvest Gold: Wealth Magick of Pumpkin Spice Commerce

The Magick of Christmas Lights: Illuminating Holiday Rituals

Cranberry Crown: Royal Self-Worth through Ritual Meals
Petosiris and the Worms of the Feathered Throne
The Evergreen Equation: Self-Help for Sustained Growth
The Rain Will Wash Us Away: Emo Weather Magick
Snowlight Shadows: Magick Under Frozen Stars
Doctor Who: Merger of Empires
The Light Within the Feast: Magickal Wealth of Yuletide Flame
Momentum Machines: Small Habits Designed to Snowball into Unstoppable Forward Motion
Calm Spells: Magickal Solutions for Anxiety Relief
Santa's Final List: The Naughty Never Leave
The Mystic's Guide to Banishing Worry
The Silence Dividend: Turning Quiet Mornings into Compounding Growth All Year
Charmed Stillness: Rituals to Ease the Mind
Blood Spiral Ascension
The Vanishing Heart Invocation
Crystal Calm: Harnessing Stones for Anxiety
The Nano Tyrant Code: Strength in the Small Predator
The Energy Ledger: Accounting Methods for Vitality, Not Just Money
Snowglobe Mindset: Shake Up Your Thoughts, Settle Into Peace
The Weight of the Feather: Anubis's Codes for Soul Balance
Pocket Peppermint Power: Tiny Rituals for Big Holiday Energy
Shadowkeeper of the Golden Jackal: Anubis's Path to Energetic Protection
The Witch's Breath: Anxiety Relief Through Magickal Breathing
The Tiny Ember: Pocket Motivation for Cold Days

Stocking Sorcery: Mini Spells for Holiday Luck and Prosperity

Warm Hands, Steady Heart: Micro Grounding for Winter Anxiety

The Jackal's Lantern: Guide-Lights for Walking the Dark Path

Anubis's Silent Steps: Rituals for Stealth, Peace & Emotional Quiet

The Bonewake Protocol

Extinction-Proof: How to Outlive Trends, Trauma, and Time

The Fourth Doctor: The Eccentric Wanderer

The Second Doctor: Chaos and Charm in the TARDIS (Patrick Troughton, 1966–1969)

The Third Doctor: Earthbound Defender of Time (Jon Pertwee, 1970–1974)

The First Doctor: Genesis of the Time Lord (William Hartnell, 1963–1966)

The Fourth Doctor: The Eccentric Wanderer *(Tom Baker, 1974–1981)*

The Fifth Doctor: Elegance and Empathy (Peter Davison, 1982–1984)

The Sixth Doctor: A Kaleidoscope of Conflict (Colin Baker, 1984–1986)

The Seventh Doctor: The Strategist of Shadows (Sylvester McCoy, 1987–1989)

The Eighth Doctor: A Time Lord's Renaissance (Paul McGann, 1996)

The War Doctor: A Time Lord's Burden (John Hurt, 2013)

The Ninth Doctor: The Healer of Worlds
(Christopher Eccleston, 2005)

The Tenth Doctor: The Lonely Hero (David Tennant, 2005–2010)

The Eleventh Doctor: The Madman in a Box (Matt Smith, 2010–2013)

The Twelfth Doctor: The Rebel with a Cause (Peter Capaldi, 2013–2017)

The Thirteenth Doctor: Breaking the Mold
(Jodie Whittaker, 2017–2022)

The Fourteenth Doctor: A New Beginning (David Tennant, 2022–2023)

The Fifteenth Doctor: Rewriting the Stars
(Ncuti Gatwa, 2023–2025)

Santa's Shortcut to Success: Micro Habits for a Better New Year

The Midnight Cocoa Manifesto: Comfort Rituals for Hard Nights

Why I Can't Save: Trauma Blocks to Financial Planning

Dino Brain, Mega Goals: Rewire Yourself for Savage Success.

Jurassic Profit: Unearth Your Inner Millionaire Fossil

Scales & Softness: Dating with Dino Heart

Carnotaurus Dreams.

Red Willow Thinking.

Reindeer Resilience: How to Keep Going When You're Exhausted

Candlewick Courage: Lighting Strength in Dark Seasons.

Elf-Mode Focus: Fast Attention Fixes for Busy Seasons

Futureproof Feelings: Emotional Skill-Building for Resilience No Matter What the New Year Brings

The 90-Day Rewire: Transform Your Neural Pathways Before Spring Blooms

Jolly Rich: Christmas Micro-Money Magick for Fast Prosperity.

Gingerbread Gratitude: Mini Practices for a Happier Holiday

Trauma-Spending: When Money Becomes a Drug

Goal Skeletons: Build Minimalist Frameworks for Resolutions That Last

The Snarl Strategy: Growling Back at a World That Silenced You

The Hourglass Reset: Reclaiming What the Clock Took

Yule Claw: Dino Rites of Light in the Darkness

Sacred Circles: Grounding Rituals for Anxious Souls

Clockstopper's Gut: Rebuilding the Core of Time

Winterfire Drive: Harness the Cold Season's Stillness to Ignite Deep Motivation

The 5-Minute Productivity Hack: Small Steps to Big Results

Light Ascending: A Self-Help Guide to Longer Days

Inner Economy: Trade Self-Doubt for Confidence Like a High-Value Currency

Simple Success: Decluttering Your Life for Better Results

The Resilient Mind: Thriving in Tough Times

The 2026 Playbook: Mastering the Year Ahead

The Spring Sleep Solution: Conquering Fatigue After Time Change.

The Hormonal Compass: Navigate Back to Your Youth

Golden Vision: Eating for Your Eye Color with the Power of Ghee

Lionhearted Love: Strength in Relationships

MiB Mindset: Think Like a Cosmic Agent

The Ladder of Small Wins: Climb Out of Stagnation by Stacking Micro-Victories

The Momentum Hour: Gaining More in Less Time.

The Year of You: A Self-Help Blueprint for Unapologetic Self-Ownership

The Dust That Watches You Back.

The Astral Parent

Shadow of the King: The Nanotyrannus Parable

Tiny Tidings of Triumph: Small Wins That Change Your Life

Dwarf Tyrant Rising: When You're the One They Overlook

The Bank Account Mirror: Healing How You See Yourself Through Money

Cretaceous Black

When Love Costs Too Much: Romantic Triggers and Financial Wounds

Dream-Eater's Guide to Wealth

Unzipped Reality: The Jacket That Opens Portals

The Power of No: How to Set Boundaries and Get Rich

Keeper of the Desert Veil: Anubis's Teachings on Illusion & Truth

Redacted Stargates: Stories the SGC Buried

The Clock That Dripped Time

Doctor Who: The Silent Acquisition

Hairline Manifestation: Unlocking Power at the Edge of Thought

Cash-Eater Crickets: How Insects Predict Economic Collapse

Dead Pet Whisperer: Grief Alchemy from the Other Side

The Love Algorithm Is Broken: Hack Romance Before It Hacks You

The Rite of the 8-Limbed Seal

Melt the Moon: A Fire Ritual to Reshape Emotion

Venomous Miracles: Healing Through the Poison Path

Wealth Without Water: The Post-Aquatic Rich Life

The Butterfly Betrayal: When Change Turns on You

The Quiet Upgrade: How Humans Are Secretly Rebuilding Themselves Without Asking Permission

Nobody Taught Us This: The Missing Human Manual for Money, Energy, and Self-Respect

You Were Never Broken: Why Most People Are Reacting Normally to an Unstable World

After the Noise Ends: How Humans Reset When the World Finally Goes Quiet

The Month That Tells the Truth: Why January Reveals What the Rest of the Year Hides

Tremors Party Unleashed: The Ultimate Guide to a Graboids Birthday Bash

Cold Start Human: Rebooting Motivation Without Forcing Momentum

The Year that doesn't start until they say

Love Without Performance: What Connection Looks Like When No One Is Watching

February Is a Mirror: What Love Exposes About You

How We Learned Love Wrong: Uninstalling Cultural Myths About Connection

You Are Not Too Much: Why Needing Love Is Not a Flaw

The Crooked Fence Covenant: Backwoods Boundaries and Witch Wealth

The Day That Keeps Repeating: Why Your Life Feels Stuck—and How to Shift It Gently

Nothing Changes Until Something Softens: Escaping Repetition Without Violence to Yourself

Same Life, Different Ending: How Tiny Choices Rewrite Repetition

The Loop Isn't Punishment: Why You're Being Asked to Learn, Not Suffer

Panic at the Register: Retail Anxiety and Public Shame

The Secret Formula to Becoming an Influencer in 90 Days

The New Rich: How to Retire by 35

Digital Nomad Secrets: How to Travel the World and Make Millions

Burn Your Waiting Room: Escape the Delay Spiral

Strapped for Pleasure: A Complete Guide to Pegging and Strap-On Play

Locked in Desire: A Guide to Chastity Play and Intimate Control

Burrowing into History: Groundhog Day Through the Ages
The Shadow Forecast: The Science of Groundhog Day
Choice Cascades: How One Decision in January Sets Ripples for the Whole Year
The Anti-Anxiety Blueprint: Mastering Fear and Stress for Success
The Ancestral Path of the Jackal Priest
Winterborn Titans: Giants of Ice and Stone
The Extinction Spire
The Emotion That Made Me Millions
Delete Their Voice: Become Unreachable
The Frostbound Mysteries: Mythical Beings of January's Chill
The Roar Within: Unlocking Your Potential
From Burrow to Sky: Groundhog Day Explained
The Boogey Book: Festive Ward-Off Edition
Fooled Ya! The Psychology Behind Great Pranks
April Fools' Alchemy: Transforming Everyday Items into Pranks
Anchor Habits: Root Yourself in Unshakable Routines That Endure Seasonal Change
Emerald Waters: A St. Patrick's Day Survival Guide for Diabetes Insipidus
The Groundhog's Legacy: Myths, Legends, and Facts
Six Weeks of Mystery: The Truth Behind Groundhog Day
The Upgrade Mind: Tech-Like Patches and Updates for Your Mental Operating System
Moon Blood, Star Flesh: Embracing Your Hybrid Nature
Groundhog Lore and Legend: A Complete Guide
You Are the Lie They Can't Kill
Download a Different Reality
The Quiet Advantage: Winning Without Announcing Yourself
A Year of Gratitude: Unlocking Joy

Touch Grass: A Pagan Reset for a Burned-Out Digital World
Cold Start Wealth: Building Financial Power from a Standing Still Point
Astrology Without Fate: Using Cycles Without Surrendering Control
The Future is Remote: Work Less, Earn More, Live Anywhere
Harvest of Silence
The Algorithm Knows Your Name
April Fools' Day for Introverts
Soft Power Systems: Influence That Doesn't Exhaust You
Practical Magick for Real Life: Focus, Intent, and Follow-Through
January Is a Lie: Designing Momentum Without the Calendar
Universal Flow: Managing DI in High-Energy Theme Parks
Electric Allure: Exploring Erotic Electro-Play
The Masked Embrace: Exploring Sensory Deprivation
The Ultimate April Fools' Survival Guide
Splashproof Survival: Waterparks & Wave Pools with DI
Agile Predator, Still King: Crafting Your Speed in a World That Celebrates Size
The Shadow Feast: Groundhog Day's Sinister Side
The Bug's Business Model
Edge of Bliss: Mastering the Art of Tease and Denial
Midnight Alchemy: Rituals for Transformation Between the Old Year and the New
Punxsutawney Bloodlines: A Groundhog Day Horror
The Burrower: Groundhog Day's Darkest Secrets
Buried Alive: A Groundhog Day Horror Story
Blood Moon Markets: The Witch's Guide to Wealth Magick
The Groundhog's Shadow: What It Means for the World
Seasonal Shadows: The Groundhog Day Phenomenon
The Shadow's Curse: A Groundhog Day Horror Tale
Punxsutawney Revealed: A Guide to Groundhog Day

Safari Hydration: Zoo & Wildlife Park Survival for DI
The Foolproof Prank Planner
***Latex Lust: Embracing Fetish Fashion* is a sophisticated**
Whip & Whisper: The Dynamics of Impact Play
The Shadow Burrow Chronicles: Horror Beneath the Ground
Frozen Shadows: A Groundhog Day Thriller
The Groundhog's Revenge: A February Nightmare
Burrow of the Damned
Everyday Enchantment: Magickal Practices for Modern Living

www.ingramcontent.com/pod-product-compliance
Lightning Source LLC
LaVergne TN
LVHW022016200926
848481LV00007B/2414
* 9 7 9 8 2 9 5 5 5 7 7 8 1 *